W9-CDI-195

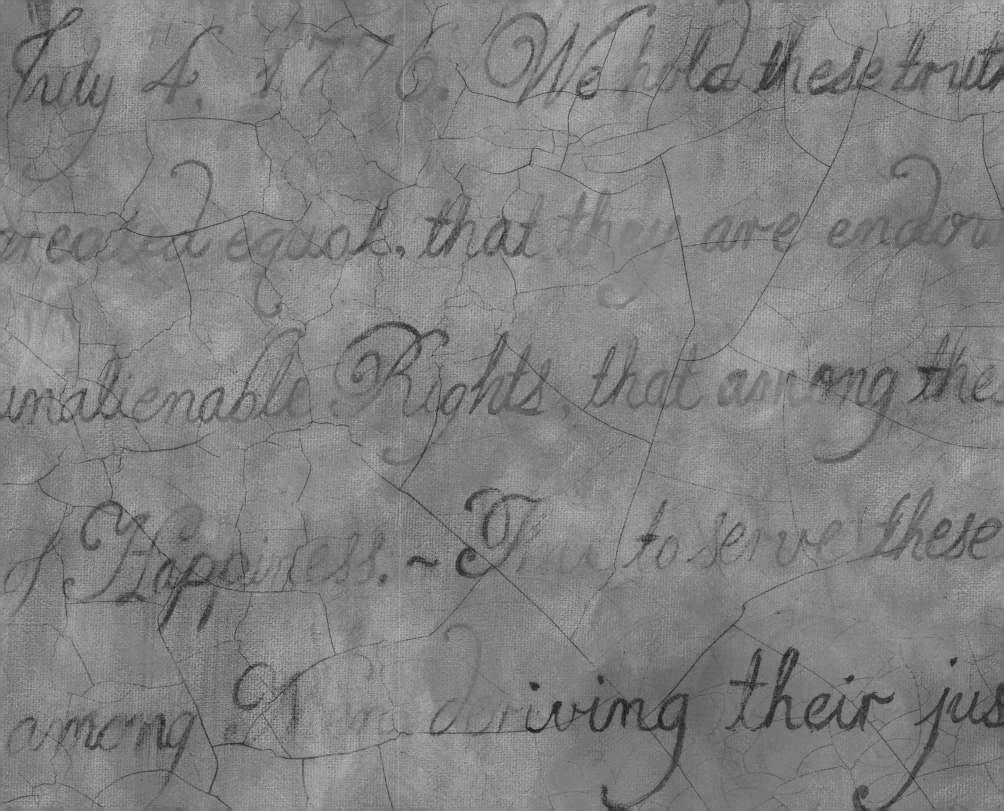

be self-evident that all men are
by their Creator with certain
Life, Liberty and the pur
Governments are instituted
powers from the consent of the g

THEY CALLED HER

Molly
Pitcher

by Anne Rockwell ❧ illustrated by Cynthia von Buhler

Alfred A. Knopf 🐎 New York

In 1777, a barber named William Hays

closed up shop and set off for Valley Forge, Pennsylvania.

He wouldn't be powdering any wigs or shaving whiskers for a while. Most of his customers had gone to fight in the War of Independence, which had broken out two years earlier between the North American colonists and the King of England. William wanted to do his part against that pigheaded king, who was denying American colonists the citizens' rights they would have had in England. So now he was going to be a soldier, too.

When he went off to join General George Washington's Colonial Army at Valley Forge, his young wife, Mary, nicknamed Molly, went with him. No one ever said she was pretty, but she was strong, hard-working, and good-natured.

General George Washington was commander in chief of the Continental Army. He and other officers, plus a bedraggled army of about 12,000 men and boys, were camped at Valley Forge just before Christmas of 1777. Snow lay deep on the ground, and Washington's troops had run out of everything they needed to keep on fighting. Washington begged the Second Continental Congress for food and supplies, but none came.

It was so cold that soldiers had to stand on their hats in the snow to keep their feet from freezing. Their shoes had holes in them from tramping over miles of rough and stony ground. They had no blankets or warm clothes. They didn't have enough to eat. Their camp was a filthy mess. Many of them were very sick. Every day, more and more soldiers deserted. Others died.

Molly and other women who'd followed husbands, sons, fathers, and brothers to Valley Forge did whatever they could to help. They cooked and cleaned, washed and mended clothes, and nursed the sick. But no matter what they did, more soldiers died each day.

Things began to look up when the Second Continental Congress finally sent supplies. General Washington began planning to go to battle again.

In late February, a German-speaking man arrived at Valley Forge. His name was Friedrich Wilhelm Augustus von Steuben and he claimed to be a baron from Prussia. He also said he'd been an officer in the army of his king, Frederick the Great. He bragged that he could turn Washington's ragtag army into a fine fighting force—as fine as those in his native Prussia, which he insisted were far better than those of the King of England.

Washington's men had been fighting the way they hunted deer or bear. They'd sneak up from behind and catch the enemy off guard. They were good at this guerrilla warfare, for they knew secret hiding places in caves and paths through woods and fields that the British didn't. But they didn't know how to fight on an open battlefield against a superbly trained, well-equipped, professional army. And Washington knew that was what they'd soon face.

The King of England had sent his finest soldiers across the sea to put down the revolution. More were on their way. Washington knew how to plan and carry out surprise attacks. That's why the British called him "that wily old fox." But he didn't see how the men and boys in his army could learn in less than two months what England's professional soldiers had spent most of their lives learning. It was impossible.

Still, he told Baron von Steuben to do the best he could.

omehow von Steuben did the impossible, and without speaking a word of English.

He taught the soldiers to face straight ahead when marching in file, rifles to their shoulder. He taught them to advance against the enemy in proper formation, for that was the way their enemies fought. He even taught the soldiers to keep their camp clean and neat, as all military camps were supposed to be. And when this happened, fewer members of the army became sick.

Molly watched and listened, and didn't forget a bit of what she saw and heard.

When they left Valley Forge late in the spring of 1778, the Continental Army was ready to fight. Its soldiers marched in single or double file, eyes straight ahead, muskets at their shoulders.

Most of them, including George Washington, said good-bye to the women who'd joined them at Valley Forge. But William Hays didn't. When he marched toward the colony of New Jersey, his wife followed.

Molly figured she'd find ways to make herself useful. She always had. She carried few possessions, but among them was a dented pewter pitcher that would prove to be one of the Americans' greatest assets.

At the end of June, a scout brought news. A large number of British soldiers, led by Sir Henry Clinton, were gathered at Monmouth Courthouse, near the New Jersey shore. The fight everyone had been preparing for was coming very soon.

Washington ordered General Charles Lee to lead an advance guard of 5,000 soldiers to attack the British. He'd send in a rear guard of more men soon after the fighting was under way.

William Hays was among Lee's advance guard marching to battle. As she always had, Molly followed.

Winter at Valley Forge had been bitter cold, but June of 1778 in New Jersey was hotter than anyone could remember.

It was just after sunrise when American soldiers fired on the British near Monmouth Courthouse. Molly could see that the day was going to be a scorcher. Heat and humidity were already shimmering up from the ground. She decided what her job would be that day.

She'd spotted a green and mossy place where a spring gushed up. She ran and filled her pitcher with cold water. She raced back to the battlefield, dodging cannon and musket fire, carrying her pitcher full of water for any American soldier who needed a drink.

The Americans knew all about such hot and humid summer days. They knew they had to keep cool any way they could. They ignored what Baron von Steuben had taught them about looking neat and military at all times. They stripped off coats, belts, wigs, hats, boots, shoes, and stockings and tossed them onto the grass.

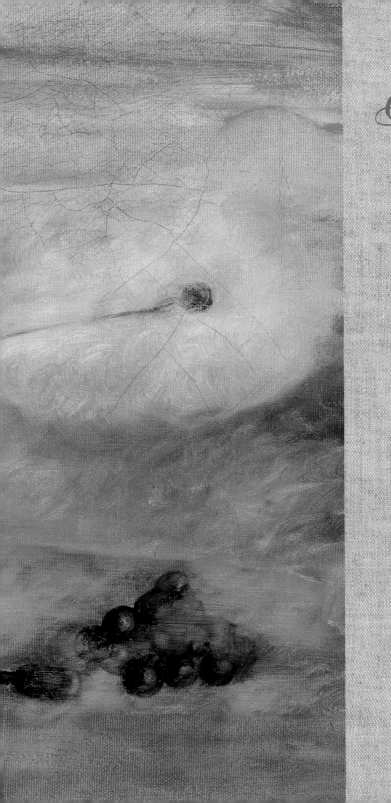

Smoke, noise, and the smell of gunpowder filled the air. Molly paid no attention. All morning, she ran back and forth from battlefield to spring, spring to battlefield, bringing water to men who'd collapsed in the heat. Over and over she heard the urgent cry of

"Molly—Pitcher!"

Still more British soldiers, under orders from Lord Cornwallis, marched toward Monmouth Courthouse. The men formed a line of scarlet like a winding river of blood. They were a magnificent and terrifying sight. But their fine uniforms weren't what they should have been wearing in the sun that blazed down on them.

Each man wore a tall black fur hat; a scarlet coat of thick, warm wool; a wide and shining black belt that held a sharp sword; a white waistcoat; and matching woolen pants with knee-high, brightly polished black boots. Each marched with his eyes straight ahead, a musket on his shoulder, a knapsack full of heavy lead balls of ammunition on his back. They moved to the stirring music of war. Drums were beating, fifes were playing, trumpets were sounding.

The soldiers started dropping as the sun rose higher. These Englishmen had never felt such heat in their home across the sea. It was almost a hundred degrees in New Jersey that day. Men grew faint and dizzy, and fell to the ground. But their companions went on marching. They never stopped or broke step, even when one man or more collapsed. Fifty-six British soldiers died of heat stroke that day.

That didn't stop them, though. All morning, more and more scarlet coats marched onto the field. Many American soldiers panicked at the sight of so many. General Lee couldn't maintain order. His soldiers forgot all about fighting in the disciplined ways Baron von Steuben had taught them. Instead, they ran in terror this way and that, hiding in ditches, up in apple trees, beneath hedges.

General Lee was sure there'd be a massacre of his troops before morning turned to noon. He gave orders to retreat.

Molly saw that some of the men, including William, disobeyed the order and kept on fighting. The sun was growing hotter. As long as any member of the Continental Army needed water to drink, Molly Hays wasn't going anywhere.

On one of her trips to the spring, she stumbled over the body of an American soldier. She assumed he was dead until she heard him moan.

The British were advancing quickly, guns aimed straight at their foes. Molly knew she could run to safety, but the wounded man couldn't walk, let alone run. He lay directly in the line of fire and would surely be killed if he stayed there.

He was a good-sized fellow, but Molly wasted no time wondering how she'd do what she had to. She picked the man up, slung him over her shoulder, and ran to a clump of bushes away from the gunfire. She laid him down there on the grass in the shade.

She ran back toward the spring and passed the cannon William was firing just in time to see a ball from a British musket hit him. William fell to the ground. She examined her husband's wound and saw that he wouldn't die from it, but he couldn't fire his cannon.

Someone had to.

Molly grabbed the long ramrod, plunged it into the barrel of the cannon, and fired it off. She kept on firing.

ball fired low from a British musket came whizzing straight toward Molly. She quickly spread her legs wide. The musket ball passed between them. It never touched her, but her skirt and petticoat were ripped and became a good deal shorter than they had been.

She muttered that it could have been worse and went back to work firing the cannon.

Soon General Washington galloped onto the field riding Nelson, his fine horse who never shied at the noise of guns or cannons, no matter how close they were. Washington carried the flag of commander in chief—thirteen stars in a circle on a field of blue silk. The flag fluttered and flew above the smoke of battle. It wasn't as bright as the scarlet coats the British soldiers wore, but to everyone who'd stayed on to fight, it was a cheering and glorious sight.

For the rest of that hot and steamy day, the Continental Army fought the way Baron von Steuben had taught it to. George Washington saw to that.

As he galloped over the battlefield, shouting orders and spurring his men on, he was amazed to catch a glimpse of a woman. She was blurred by the smoke that surrounded her. Her face was smudged with gunpowder and sweat. But George Washington saw her take a deep breath, then run and shove the long ramrod into the big gun with as much force as possible. The cannon boomed. The explosion shook the ground, but the woman paid no attention— she just got ready to fire the cannon again.

When the sun set, the fighting stopped. Neither side could go on in darkness. Exhausted British and American soldiers put down their guns and tended to their dead and wounded. Late that night, they sat down to eat and rest, to prepare themselves for another day of fighting.

That same night, General Washington asked some of his officers about the woman he'd seen firing a cannon. He listened to what they said about how she'd carried water through the gunfire to the soldiers all that morning.

Washington ordered that the woman be brought before him. He told her she'd been as brave in battle as any man he'd ever heard of. He decided she'd earned the rank of sergeant in the Continental Army.

As she listened to what the tall, strong general said, Molly Hays had never felt so proud in her life.

No man who heard General Washington speak to her that night doubted that Molly had earned her rank. As the news spread through the troops, no soldier sneered at the thought of a woman being a sergeant in *his* army, even though no one present had ever heard of such a thing.

That night, Sergeant Molly Hays lay down on the grass at the edge of the field beside William and the rest of the soldiers of the Continental Army. Long after the stars filled the sky, General George Washington spread his cape over the grass, tied Nelson to a tree, and lay down with his weary soldiers.

As he lay gazing up at the stars, planning his strategy for the next day's battle, fires danced on the hill across the field where the British were camped. The voices of many men carried through the night. Sentries marched back and forth, keeping their endless watch. It was very late before everything was quiet except for the chorus of frogs singing in the nearby swamp.

Molly and the other American soldiers rose before the sun. They'd had some sleep and were ready to fight again. Many believed they could win.

But they didn't fight the British that day. No scarlet-coated soldiers marched onto the field. They'd gone away.

Sir Henry Clinton and Lord Cornwallis had ordered a retreat. They didn't want their men to fight that wily old fox again this morning. They were afraid they'd lose. Washington's Continental Army didn't fight like farmers, as the British leaders had been sure they would. They fought like soldiers. And one of those soldiers was a woman.

o one knows if Sergeant Molly Hays took part in any of the battles that followed. By the time the British surrendered and the war ended in 1783, she and William had gone home to Carlisle, Pennsylvania.

Molly went back to the same work she'd done before the war—doing laundry, cleaning houses, and taking care of children. The only fault her employers ever found with her was that she swore like a soldier.

In 1789, George Washington was elected the first president of a new country, the United States of America. No longer would the American people have to obey a faraway king. They had won the battle to become a free and independent nation. And one of the people who helped win this freedom was Molly Hays.

Soldiers who'd fought at the Battle of Monmouth never forgot her. They told their children and grandchildren about the brave woman who'd been in the battle with them. They told how she'd run through gunfire again and again that hot day to bring them the drink of cool and refreshing water that kept them fighting. They called her Molly Pitcher. And that's the name we remember her by. But she never called herself that. As long as she lived, she asked everyone to call her Sergeant Molly.

The Battle of Monmouth

Author's Note

Ever since I was a child, I've loved the story of Molly Pitcher. I loved her feisty, no-nonsense courage and self-reliance at the Battle of Monmouth. These seem to me exactly the traits that guaranteed the American colonists would win their war against the stubborn, unreasonable, but nevertheless far more powerful King of England. Adaptability like Molly Pitcher's is something the American people have always relied upon in crisis. And it was certainly called upon in this battle that ended in the founding of a new and strong nation.

Legends tell people a lot about who they are and how they became that way. The story of the woman at the Battle of Monmouth quickly spread by word of mouth and filled people's imaginations. It became a beloved legend of the new American nation. But unlike some legends, this one is historically true.

There has been some misunderstanding about who Molly Pitcher actually was. For a long time, she was assumed to be a certain Mary Ludwig from Pennsylvania, who married a man named John Hays. Therefore, Molly Pitcher is referred to in some books as Mary Ludwig Hays. But John Hays was never listed as a member of the artillery in 1778, a gunner at the Battle of Monmouth. A man named William Hays, married to another Mary whose maiden name is unknown, was. This Mary Hays married another man after William's death and became Mary Hays McCauly.

The most useful information I was able to find on Mary Hays McCauly came from the United States Field Artillery Association in Fort Sill, Oklahoma, which awards a medal called the Artillery Order of Molly Pitcher. It is awarded by a field artillery commander to those who have "voluntarily contributed in a significant way to the improvement of the field artillery community."

Molly Pitcher, or Mary Hays McCauly, lived a long life and is buried in Carlisle, Pennsylvania, where a monument has been erected to her.

In **1765**, England passed laws taxing the American colonies without their consent, and resentment of King George III grew to the point of rebellion.

Here are some important events in the resulting struggle for American independence.

1770 – The Boston Massacre: A skirmish between British troops and a crowd in Boston leads to open fire in which four civilians (among them Crispus Attucks, a black sailor and former slave) are killed.

1773 – The Boston Tea Party: American patriots, disguised as Mohawk Indians, throw 342 chests of tea overboard in the Boston Harbor, protesting the king's tax on it and the many other taxes he has imposed.

1775 – The Midnight Ride of Paul Revere: On April 18, 1775, Paul Revere warns the patriots of the British troops' approach.

1775 – The Shot Heard Around the World: Shots fired at the battles of Lexington and Concord on April 19, 1775, mark the official beginning of the U.S. War of Independence.

1776 – Declaration of Independence: On July 4, 1776, the Declaration of Independence is approved by the Continental Congress and separates the thirteen American colonies from England.

1776 – Washington Crosses the Delaware: On December 25, 1776, after having been driven to the western bank of the Delaware River, Washington leads his troops across the river to Trenton for a surprise attack on the British.

1777 – The Winter at Valley Forge: On December 19, 1777, after losses at Brandywine and Germantown, General George Washington leads 12,000 soldiers to this winter encampment in Pennsylvania. The soldiers survive a harsh winter, but morale improves as they learn new drilling methods.

1778 – Battle of Monmouth: On June 28, 1778, this decisive battle, in which Molly Pitcher plays a part, is fought; this is the first battle after Valley Forge.

1781 – Victory at Yorktown: On October 19, 1781, Lord Cornwallis, general of the British Army, surrenders more than 7,000 men to George Washington at Yorktown, Virginia. Fighting ends and the war is won.

1783 – Independence!: On September 3, 1783, the Treaty of Paris is signed. Great Britain officially recognizes the United States' independence.

For my granddaughter, Julianna Joy Brion,
whose birthday is also Flag Day—A.R.

For Adam Buhler, Xavier Dietrich II, Kate Gartner,
and for all of the Carrozza family women and our little girls:
Gabrielle, Claire, and Katie—C.v.B.

With special thanks to Richard S. Walling,
Dr. Garry Wheeler Stone, Dan Silvich, and Gary Saretzky
for their expert advice.

Cynthia von Buhler created the illustrations in this book using oil paints on
stretched linen canvas. She then applied a crackle glaze and burnished the
paintings with a sepia tone to give the appearance of age.

THIS IS A BORZOI BOOK PUBLISHED BY ALFRED A. KNOPF

Text copyright © 2002 by Anne Rockwell
Illustrations copyright © 2002 by Cynthia von Buhler
All rights reserved under International and Pan-American Copyright Conventions. Published in the United States of America by Alfred A. Knopf, a division of Random House, Inc., New York,
and simultaneously in Canada by Random House of Canada Limited, Toronto. Distributed by Random House, Inc., New York. KNOPF, BORZOI BOOKS, and the colophon are registered trademarks of Random House, Inc.

www.randomhouse.com/kids

Library of Congress Cataloging-in-Publication Data
Rockwell, Anne F.
They called her Molly Pitcher / by Anne Rockwell ; illustrated by Cynthia von Buhler.
p.   cm.
ISBN 0-679-89187-0 (trade) — ISBN 0-679-99187-5 (lib. bdg.) 1. Pitcher, Molly, 1754–1832—Juvenile literature. 2. Monmouth, Battle of, 1778—Juvenile literature. 3. Women revolutionaries—United States—
Biography—Juvenile literature. 4. Revolutionaries—United States—Biography—Juvenile literature. 5. United States—History—Revolution, 1775–1783—Biography—Juvenile literature. [1. Pitcher, Molly, 1754–1832.
2. Revolutionaries. 3. United States—History—Revolution, 1775–1783. 4. Monmouth, Battle of, 1778. 5. Women—Biography.] I. Buhler, Cynthia von, ill. II. Title.

E241.M7 R63 2002
973.3'092—dc21
[B]   2001029422

Printed in the United States of America
May 2002
First Edition
10 9 8 7 6 5 4 3 2 1

December 15. 1791. We the P

...to form a more perfect Union...

Tranquility. provide for the common...

...and secure the Blessings of Lib...

...ordain and establish this Constitution...

e of United States, in Order

Justice, to insure domestic

fence, promote the general Welfare

ourselves and our Posterity, do

or the United States of America